FABER NE

IN THE SAME SERIES

Rachel Curzon

FABER & FABER

First published in 2016
by Faber & Faber Ltd
Bloomsbury House
74–77 Great Russell Street
London WC1B 3DA

Typeset by Hamish Ironside
Printed in England by Abbeystar

ACKNOWLEDGEMENTS

With many thanks to *The Rialto*, to the judges of the Poetry London
and Bridport Prize competitions, and to the Society of Authors
for an Eric Gregory Award in 2007.

A CIP record for this book
is available from the British Library

ISBN 978-0-571-33042-3

2 4 6 8 10 9 7 5 3 1

Contents

Hydra

1

I have not brought everything I need.
There are books I would like to have beside me.
They ask me: which books would make you happy
and we will fetch them. I cannot recall
the titles, or who wrote them.

2

When I stepped down onto the platform
I pretended to look for somebody I knew.

3

Water here comes in paper cups like paper cones.
What seems plentiful soon diminishes.
I am still able to think like this.

4

Whatever they tell you, the sky is particular.
There is no one looking at the moon
just at this moment and thinking of me
but if there were, I would lean out above the quiet street
and shout *anyway it is the wrong moon.*

5

I have spoken my own name
exactly fourteen times since I arrived.
Now it is nothing but a sound.

It always was just a sound.

6

Tiles (floor): terracotta, rough-edged, ridged.
Tiles (wall): ceramic. Occasional pansies.
I would like to lay something against me
and find it fits precisely.

7

I painted a picture with my fingers.
I told them it was my mother.

They took it from me before the paint was dry.
Draw a nice house, now, they told me.

8

I find plenty to do every day
so why is it
that the pages of my diary are white?

9

There is a road out of the village.
It would be so easy to leave.
I go a little way, but stop. Turn back.
I will not lead myself astray.

Postcard

I walked out into a new place –
felt sure that I was here to learn things –
waited for them to come, pulling at grasses.

The cabbage whites might tell me something –
there were so many of them, all hectic.
They said *it is terribly simple.*
But I watched them bumping through the gorse
and couldn't trust them.

I looked up, looked out – somebody had said I should –
and the hills said *magnificence*
the fields said *warp and weft*
the road said *certain.*

I could understand none of them
and so I held myself very still
and waited for something to love me – just enough.

But all around, the trees said *lightning*
the turf said *footfall*
the house said *the indifference of sons.*

The land grew darker as it stepped away.
Its edges became clouds.

Advice from Marianne Davies in which She Expounds upon the Perils of Mr Franklin's Glass Armonica

Beware the glass armonica.
It is a charmed, insinuating thing
that you might treasure as a novelty.
Approach it cautiously.

Yes, it is a fragile instrument.
A clumsy move could smash it
in an instant – yet its tune will curl
a pretty scarf about your throat
and drag you gently from the world.

How will you know it?
Listen for a sound like the North Star
or a sound like the pale eyes of wolves.
It will remind you of the cold that settles
on a house when all the promises have cracked
to let a kind of winter in.

And when you are adept
at spinning music from this toy,
you will understand
that there is nothing else but this
for all the life to come –

Accomplishments.
French windows leading
from the morning room.
Charming hothouse flowers
and safe encounters
with acceptable gentlemen.

Master

There was music wherever you turned.
In every vestibule, somebody playing a piano.
I never used to like the sound of a cor anglais
but it has grown on me. I started to wonder
what I would play if I had my time again.
Perhaps I was waiting for a man in tweed
to stop me in the corridor and offer me a cello.
To physically bar my way with a cello
until I agreed to handle the bow, and at that
he would spring away, satisfied. He would move
noddingly off, leaving me fingering the horsehair,
impatient to be a virtuoso. Yes, I might have been a cellist.

I began to hum while marking papers alone.
I acquired that habit. I would hum my way quietly
across the pitches at dusk, I would hum my way around corners,
and surprise boys in knee socks, also humming.
We were never humming the same melody.
Wouldn't that have been remarkable.

The view of the cathedral was quite splendid.
I have always enjoyed crocketed pinnacles
and, of course, I never had to look at my wristwatch.
Day to day, I can honestly tell you I never once looked
at my wristwatch for the purpose of telling the time.
Bells, bells – it was like being in Oxford.
Yes, I think it must be exactly like studying at Magdalen,
leaning out of open windows into the sound of bells.
I acquired sepia ink and emerald ink
and I placed the bottles at opposite ends of my desk.
I stationed myself between two high-quality inks.

When it snowed, no one was permitted
to walk across the quad. The boys clamoured for snowmen.
Oh, they were quite impossible for snowmen.
They did their best, of course, scraping snow from the paving,
but not one solitary boy placed so much as a toe
onto that quad. That surely stood for something.

I should have made them take the decorations away.
When they left, everything seemed tawdry.
I raged at the paper chains, I was furious with them.
All those ridiculous candy canes.
I had wasted my money.
None of them deserved a candy cane,
they were dreadful little ingrates, all of them,
leaving their sweetmeats dangling on cotton.
I listened to the bells clashing and clashing
on Christmas morning and I went very deliberately
along the row, snapping those red and white batons,
snapping them into the smallest fragments imaginable
and tossing them all into the untouched snow.

Question

I buy thoughtful presents.
When people express preferences
I remember them. Sometimes yes
I go over the top because I like to give.
People may find this extravagant
and alarming. I do not mean it.
If I had to correct your pronunciation
I would find a joking way to do it.
You would barely notice it.
Or I would incorporate the word
into a sentence of my own, correctly,
and leave it up to you.
I try to bring people in from the sidelines.
I am at my best with underdogs and misfits.
My mother would say to me,
You and your lame ducks.
Animals tend to like me.
Once, a blind dog nosed my thigh
and rested the length of its jaw in my palm.
I can tolerate long stretches alone.
I recently climbed Blencathra via Sharp Edge alone.
I was by myself when I stood in the summit ring.
If ever you are shivering, I will give you my coat.
I will push my coat around your juddering shoulders
and I will blow on your hands.
I will chafe your hands in my hands.
I like to be held after sex.

Ultrasound

She said	I'm sorry about all the pressing
I said	press away I am not delicate you can see I am not delicate
I said	it is not every day that an opportunity arises to prove resistance
	I can feel my muscles meeting your contraption
	and I can give them the smallest pulse like this
	and you are temporarily vanquished
She said	this will be cold
I said	I have always wondered how it would feel
	ever since I watched Blue Peter in 1980 in fact
	when they put jelly onto Tina's tummy and took pictures inside
	it is a clinical kind of cold not like a hypodermic needle
	but more like damp plaster on a fractured wrist
	or tea left too long by a white bedside
	it is a viscous cold like dare I say it sperm
She said	now it's your liver we're looking at isn't it
I said	if I'd had a potato peeler to hand I would have flayed
	my own skin from my flesh I would have grated the dry areas
	to something like talcum powder or wax shavings after a fancy dinner
	and the damp areas I would have skimmed off
	like labels left on crockery and helpfully washed up
	I would have pushed my skin to a greyish ridge of paste
	the itching was like torture dreamed up by the Ancient Greeks
	me and Prometheus you see how ironic my liver you see
She said	well your liver looks fine completely normal
	your spleen is completely normal

I said what is a spleen what is a spleen for
She said you've been under the weather
     now we've got you here we'll have a little look around
I said while I was waiting the door to Room 1 opened
     and a family came out I could see that Room 1 was in
      darkness
     there was something like a spaceship there was a
      monitor
     there was a chaise longue just as you see on the television
     not a chaise longue I can't think of the proper name
      for it
I said there was a woman and a man both very tall and
      a small child
     with her gilet buttoned up wrongly and there was a baby
     just the beginning of one but it existed
     they must have just met the baby met it for the first
      time perhaps
     because they were smiling and I did not exist and their
      small child
     did not exist not much existed I think but the moon-
      scape on the monitor
     and those bunched contours that incipient baby
She said deep breath please
I said press very hard indeed
I said press until you find my babies until you can see them
      all
     they must be very jolly altogether they are so patient
     it must be very festive can you see them yet
I said can you see my red-headed baby with his intimidating
      rower's thighs
     when he rows on the Cherwell I shall bring him flapjack
      in tinfoil
     I will instruct him to love his freckles I will worry
     that his leather jacket is too heavy to lug about all day
     as a medical professional tell me will it put his back
      out

She said   deep breath please
I said   can you see my reckless baby   my iconoclast
               has he insisted on remaining in the breech position   he's
                 like that
               is he ranting about Joe Strummer
She said   deep breath please
I said   my ectomorph musician baby will be busying himself
               with something important   he will consider himself
               too grand to associate with the others   his hands
               will be very expressive   you will notice his hands first
               he is a coward really   I will have to work hard to love
                 him
               now that his cowardice has made itself apparent to me
               now that the scales have fallen from my eyes   so to
                 speak
She said   deep breath please
I said   there is a fourth   perhaps he didn't make it
               he is exceptionally clever   he should have got a First
               can you see him   is he looking after himself
I said   press as hard as you can   seek them out
               all of them   they must be hiding   they are all such
                 rascals
               find them
I said   they are all boys   fancy that   I had my girls' names
               ready picked
She said   deep breath please
I said   may I have a photo for my purse   I'd like to have one
               if it's not too late
She said   you're awfully quiet there   are you alright?

Threats

I have been granted such territories.
I have made my home there carefully –
made them belong to me.
It is hard to believe –
I thought I would always wander,
a member of nothing.
Now I line up my shoes
in the same place each evening.

And I can tell no one that I lie awake,
dangerous with terror –
breathing out, breathing in –
imagining my world laid out exactly
in some grey official room
as capable women gather around it
with perfectly straight lines
down the backs of their calves,
trailing the ends of their lovely hair
across each sacred place of it.
Oh, they push their own dreams
back and forth so confidently
over my hard-won territories
with their long sticks!

Worst Winter

In which snow makes a boy of you
and leaves me cold.

In which a white walk stretches
and then shrinks to her

laughing in the picture
from behind her wet hair.

In which you help her build an igloo
and I reread the list we made:

Period (Victorian?)
2–3 bed?

Exhibit

I would like to show you my halo.
It is robust and glorious.
One spring day I put it on like this,
wanting to distinguish myself.
I felt it brace itself.
I felt the fierce band fiercer –
clutch about my head, so attentive
like a migraine.

I will be compressed to some dense absolute,
I celebrated.

And other halos arrived
because I was so very Good.
I wore one in a band about my throat.
Every time I breathed
it gave me this word: *stainless*.
I inhaled, exhaled, loving myself.

Soon my wrists earned little halos of their own,
very shiny. They always reminded me
not to point, or finger breakables,
or hold things in imprudent ways.
I moved them in sunlight
the way a confident man might shoot his cuffs
and flexed myself slightly
inside all these golden hoops.

Everybody looked at me
and none of them had halos.
I will dress always in white,
I said, very solemnly.

Now I would like to show you all of this.
I am so full of halo.
It is quite an accomplishment.
Tomorrow I will add another, another
around my curious eyes,
my careless mouth.

The Catch

I fished her from the river,
my baby, my plaything,
and pledged I'd never leave her.

She wasn't breathing
so I sang my favourite songs
into her lungs – they started moving.

Yes, I have paced about and longed
for such as this.
Don't tell me that it's wrong

to take this pretty risk –
to put her to my dripping breast
and find she fits.

You tell me I should let her rest,
let her be.   I know best.

Happy Ending

The baby in the tree has cried all day.
There is nothing to suck on, up there.

At first he shrieked at everything green
and the climbing frame
and the way wind feels
but now he has run himself out with crying and crying
and he simply creaks.

Recently the sun tried to set
but long branches held it back,
tutting a little. It's summer.
Days are meant to finish late.

Even so, the world dismantles
according to the rules.
Trains follow themselves home
and the football match is finishing.
Boys clatter their feet.

One by one, bay windows become interesting
as families show off among their cushions,
stretching and staring.

Had you forgotten the baby?
He fits a fist into his mouth
and tells a jogger on the towpath he is hungry.
In time he'll know better than to appeal to joggers
but now those rhomboid calves winking away
are the worst thing to happen to the baby . . .

Evenings are so pitiless.
The sky sits on the goalposts to wait;
rooks listen from in amongst twigs.

And here,
        here comes someone in her slippers
picking her way through the dandelions
and the quiet swings
reaching for the baby with a smile on her mouth
saying, *Now will you hush now will you?*